CW00469234

Kate Fletcher

Wild Dress
Clothing & the natural world

Uniformbooks

First published 2019
Reprinted with revisions 2021
Copyright © Kate Fletcher
ISBN 978-1-910010-21-1

Uniformbooks
7 Hillhead Terrace, Axminster, Devon EX13 5JL
www.uniformbooks.co.uk

Trade distribution in the UK by Central Books
www.centralbooks.com

Printed and bound by T J Books, Padstow, Cornwall

Contents

Preface

In July 2013 I spent nearly a fortnight on board a sailing boat, *The Lady of Avenel*, in the Western Isles of Scotland. I was both grateful and amazed to have had such an opportunity at all. There was a free space on board and no one else wanted to go. It was a bit like when I was given the role of school head girl in the late 1980s by default. In my Liverpool comp, people didn't put themselves forward for things, but I thought I'd give it a go. Aboard the *Avenel* there was a group of great people and the great animate world, like nothing I had ever seen. There was a lot to look at and so I spent hours on deck. Truth be told, I also couldn't see a thing below. In the space of two days early in the trip I went from being blissfully sharp in my focus of the world both near and far, to being completely unable to see myself in the mirror. I was suddenly, shockingly, longsighted. I couldn't put on mascara, read a word. It was caused, I think, by gazing endlessly at the distant ocean (later I found an essay from 1789 by John Adams that confirmed that this happened to many other 'journeyman sailors' before me; "those that are habituated to look at remote objects are generally long sighted, want spectacles soonest and use the deepest magnifiers"). The sky was luminous midsummer. Seabird colonies dripped from island cliffs. The ocean writhed with whirlpools and showed dolphins, phosphorescent creatures, fish. There were island silhouettes, glimpses of magical light creeping around the edges of the sky, a shifting colour palette of a waxing and waning moon. When I got over the awkwardness, I borrowed a pair of the skipper's ready specs. But the sea's legacy is, for me, a permanent, bodily reminder to look long. To look to the 'offing'—the physical place which is the distant part of the sea. To seek out other perspectives, underlying patterns, gathering relationships and subtle changes in surroundings; in order also to better understand the conditions close by. In the offing, I saw that I needed to turn my work towards nature. I saw that I needed to explore where garments and the natural world meet.

On the face of it, turning work like mine towards nature may not seem that much of a shift. For more than two decades I have been working in design, sustainability and fashion, exploring environmental impact and how to make change. I now work as a Professor at University of the Arts London, where I've done projects that look at localism, usership, slow culture. I've also designed things, made things, grown hemp, worked with brands and politicians, given talks, written quite a bit. But in the offing I saw that much of my work had circled around nature, had dealt with it obliquely, in passing, but never as its focus. I saw that I needed to relate and uncover experience of engaging with the natural world.

The texts that make up this book were written over a six year period after the boat trip. I wrote them largely in two places in the north west of England, the region I was born in and in which I now live, despite never imagining that I would return. They talk about interdependence between garments and nature as part of life and living. They see nature not as dead resource, separate from humans, a source of textile materials and the inspiration for colour and pattern; but as the self-willed participatory world which is alive, including in what we wear. Garments are separate from neither people nor nature, they work between them both, sometimes as a barrier, other times a conduit, and at other times still, a network. They can reveal possibilities, ecological limits, delight, natural knowledge, care, freedom and new hope that it is possible to make our contributions and live well in a particular place at this time with all our relations. Garments can enhance our understanding of human embeddedness in nature, our sense of relationship with everything else.

The *Wild Dress* writings are from my life. They record details as they were experienced, as I remember them. But they are not only mine. As Erika Hasebe-Ludt, Cynthia Chambers and Carl Leggo say, "The stories of our lives, if only our own stories, would not be worth telling. These stories become an ethos for our times, as they expose interdependence and interrelatedness with all the beings of the cosmos, and the necessity of compassion and generosity in sustaining those relationships."[1] It seems that they are yours as well.

For Jude and Cole, again.

1

Royal Blue

It was all of 10:00 a.m. I leant on the wooden farm gate and waved a greeting to Gordon. He is in his sixties; short, lean but with massive unkempt, mutton-chop sideburns. The top of his head is bald and nut brown, the sides of it, whiskery, pale. His ears are blackened by chilblains. He had been checking the ewes. There are about a hundred sheep on this part of Bough Fell, stretching up to the tarn, and more than twenty times that number in the total flock. Gordon is jolly, twinkly. He is shy too, like a boy. We have known each other for decades; communicating chiefly through the medium of the long-distance wave; a single turn at a barn dance thirty years ago; and the occasional fruit pie his mum would bake for us when she was alive. He lives on his own, in a house on the opposite side of the narrow Garsdale valley from where we stay and from where he and his brother farm the rough hills. I know quite a bit about him, mostly gleaned second hand from my mum, who likes to gather knowledge of others. He leaves the dale rarely. He has been on a plane twice and hated it. There is much to recommend him.

I have only ever seen one window lit at his place across the valley. It is the bright white light of a fluorescent tube, always late at night. I speculate that he lives in one room only. I hope he has a fire. Does he cook? I remember in my youth his mum used to cater at scale for her boys: entire loaves of white bread sandwiches; whole cakes; boxes of biscuits. On the stove, a pan deep in fat, waiting for something to fry. When he saw me, he cut the engine of his quad bike, climbed off and came over, a little lame. I wondered if he appraised me as I did him, seeing the passing of time. He asked about my kids and my job, where we live. His dry sense of humour turned over my answers. I asked about the sheep and the birds. When on home ground he was confident, sure of his knowledge. He laughed and with lightness translated my names for the creatures into his vernacular, and supplemented that with where they roost and how they feign an injured wing to distract attention from their nest. I struggled to keep up; the Yorkshire brogue jingled my ears.

He was dressed in a plaid cotton shirt, heavy navy working trousers and a battered royal blue quilted country-wear jacket, fastened by tarnished press-studs to the neck. The jacket was polyester. Topstitching in a diamond shape held the frayed wadding together. Its collar was corduroy, threadbare, greasy and it sat big around his throat. It spoke the life of a hill farmer: continuous toil, economy, realism and isolation. I realised I was trying to understand how it was. I noticed one of the jacket's patch pockets, with a line of red running stitches hand sewn down its edge, and complimented him on the sewing. It turned out that he had done it that morning. He had got up at six, checked the animals, gone back home—he said he was feeling tired—and then picked up a needle and set about mending his jacket. This is apparently what sheep farmers do when they are tired. The stitches were beautifully even. The red thread a sassy choice on the blue. They showed delicacy, skill, practice. I looked at his hands, grossly swollen by manual work, gnarled by the cold, by rheumatism; two nails entirely black, others cracked, split. I listened to him tell me about carrion crows, about how the number of lambs a ewe carries to full term is influenced by how high she grazes on the fell. I looked at the red stitches, worked for no one but himself. I tried to take in the whole of this place, the relationships between things, the ways in which garments are part of the community of the land.

The same royal blue of Gordon's jacket surfaced elsewhere. It was the exact colour of a friend of mine's coat in the same style as Gordon's, that she inherited from her mother forty years before. Tatty but still strong. It was also the same shade as a boxy, dense knitted polyester sweatshirt owned by my husband; the only garment from his teenage years to have stayed in his wardrobe into adult life. Only later did I realise that the wearers of all these pieces have blue eyes. I began to wonder if such things are part of the decision tree that influences the clothes we wear and hang on to. Whether it could be that blue-eyed people find a kind of fittingness, an enduring self-recognition, in blue garments? Maybe they do. Whatever it is, underneath it all it seems that there is something more basic: our actual, natural selves are ever present in what we wear. We can dress up all we like, but clothes reveal us as natural beings. They unearth our animal bodies, our self-willed breath, our responsibilities to the world. The question that then follows is what this means for how we dress; what we will do about it.

2

Socks

Black socks
they never get dirty,
The longer you wear them the cleaner they get.
Black socks
you think you should wash them,
But something inside you says oh no not yet,
Not yet, not yet…

[Sung in a round]

It was February and I was journeying north with my children, driving across a boundary on the map which marks the start of the Yorkshire Dales. The Dales' landscape and geology don't begin at the National Park sign; there's no dale end, or watershed. But I marked a change. I was happy to cross the threshold; I like it here.

As we drive, the hilltops that flank us have traces of snow, thin strips of old lace. We stopped at the tiny Spar shop at the edge of the village of Sedbergh. Outside the car, away from kids' breath and Radio 1, the air feels cold but not freezing. In our on-off winter, temperatures have yet to plummet. I go in for some messages and at the till point, in prime retail spot, is a job lot of 2.3 Tog thermal socks. Orange-red, polyester, thick pile, bundled in pairs with a band of cheap white card taped around their middle. Forget the chocolate and cheap lager that adorns the checkouts where I live. The Yorkshire Dales has different vices; socks are its weakness. Life in open ground and wind corridors fuse different things to place.

I too have some new socks, knee high with a turnover, khaki green, with a single stripe of mustard at the top. Their colour reminds me of a February field. They were a birthday present, chosen to guard the clothes underneath from mud. This is not a new idea I know, socks have long been used as instant gaiters, smaller and easier to wash than the big trouser legs underneath. My first time of wearing the socks, pulled up high over black jeans, I was flirted with by a robin. He bobbed and boldly flashed his ass. He sang, dashed forward a few metres and then back again, standing his ground. It was nice to be noticed.

The new socks are British made, 97% wool, 3% nylon to reinforce the toe and heel; a linked seam above the toe to crease in comfort. I used them often in the first few months of the year. The land was saturated, churned up, there was mud everywhere. Land that looked solid, slid away underfoot. Grass glistened, hillsides shimmered, not with usual winter conditions of frost and snow, but with running water. In the fields and paths, the mud took on the consistency of curry sauce. The mud's tones varied: melted milk chocolate, a lightly spiced chai, rusty wastewater, dark brown swill. It was slick, unctuous, a cold pyroclastic flow. Needless to say, I fell in it. The most total slip was a feet-first slide down a hill. Hands, legs, arms and shoulders, hair, covered. Mud sluiced up my back, its cold fingers stealing their way between the layers of clothing to my skin. I grinned for somehow everyone else was still upright—how had I not brought them down with me? Soon my smallest son was sucked in too, into the horizontal gloop. Left leg, from ankle to hip, back, left shoulder, hands, plastered. Hand in muddy hand, he and I wandered on, clothes turning to board in the brisk wind. We were literally layered in the landscape. Like Arnold Schwarzenegger in the camouflage scene in *Predator*, daubed.

A stiff brush worked a charm on the dry mud, dispersing it as dust around the place. As I brushed, I remembered that once when I was walking near the hamlet of Rainowlow close to where I live, I saw a man at the head of a footpath, next to his car, with a clothes brush in hand. He was grooming a woman. He was working the brush down her upper body in long strokes. The couple didn't see me at first and started as I got closer. Embarrassed, he fumbled for the car keys and she busied around at the back of the car, then they jumped in and quickly drove past me and away, forcing me into the bushy verge. It was only their reaction that made me realise that for them it was an indecent thing to have had witnessed. Caught *in flagrante*, in the act of clothes cleaning. And outdoors too.

It is so much more effective to brush a piece of clothing when it's on the body: when the sleeves and legs are full of a limb, a torso, something to work against. Often there's also a need to anchor one edge of the fabric somewhere, to peg the fabric taut, in order to create enough friction between bristle and cloth. This can be impossible if you're brushing the same sleeve that you're wearing because you also need to stretch it out. For this, three hands are the perfect number. I suggest it is best always to groom someone else. Like it's always best to get someone else to cut your hair. People pay good money for such services.

On my clothes the mud's deeper reach, tucked between a sweatshirt's knitted stitches and into the twill weave of denim, needed soaking and rubbing to cajole it out. The sink full of water darkened as I pummelled the clothes, taking on the same colour as the land outside. Of course it did. Although somehow it still surprised me. As the water drained away, the bottom of the sink was covered with earth, like after washing soily potatoes. Clothes are also, after all, a gift from the land. I didn't wash out the mud from the inside of the jumper I had been wearing. Not sure why I would bother. It will fleck off with time.

After my son and I fell in the mud, my mum said, "Wasn't our washing machine going to have its work cut out?" And I recalled that it wasn't until I was about seven that we got an automatic washing machine. Before that it was an arrangement of soaking buckets, a spin dryer, long wooden tongs and a washing line stretched across a shady concrete yard. It was an uphill battle; cold, wet, physical, graceless.

For her, mud and the world it came from increased her toil. Whereas for me, one generation on, with all my privileges, I have found a way to make peace with it. This muddy world is my house, and it is keeping me.

Four months on, and we moved to a cottage without a washing machine. I then laundered much less. In fact I came to know that there is always another day of wear to be had from every dirty garment. I extended my repertoire of clothes brushes. I aired things often. I ignored small stains. Habitual, casual, tossing of clothes in the laundry basket became a fruitless activity; they didn't emerge again any time soon. Among other things, the weekly trip to the launderette made conspicuous the choices and actions that convenience hides from view.

When I did go there, I liked the launderette; it was very sociable. My local one was run by two women from Liverpool, and my own scouse accent grew and danced more with every load. They would ask me to help them fold bed sheets. They told me thin towels are best. They gave me advice about my hair. They took hand washing home as a favour for others who couldn't manage it. Folding and talking, ceaselessly moving piles of clothes through the system, they praised my kids for unloading the big machine, for being children who knew how to work. They scolded them for fiddling with dials, for playing with a tennis ball inside. A few times I took some mending with me and fixed things as I waited for the washing machine to finish its cycle. Regulars came and went, some came and sat, absorbing the warmth of the tumble driers. A few people dropped off duvets that needed washing in a larger machine than the one they had at home. These people stuck out, they were unfamiliar with the launderette's dynamics and exchange, with filling a machine, with coin slots, with the banter, with waiting in turn. The British launderette is a place of old school class divisions, of gender gaps, of informal social care, pet sitting and a lift to the hospital. I think it was how working men's clubs used to operate. But this launderette was run by women with bags of dirty clothes, who would help you if you were in need.

I manhandled our bag of wet washing back home and hung it up to dry at Woodcutter's Cottage, the house we were renting on a smallholding next to a forest. Outside I strung up a washing line from a post and attached the other end to a farm trailer and then criss-crossed other lengths to a young sycamore tree. I tried pegging out the laundry in other places, but it seemed that wherever I did, birds landed on the line, a handy perch, and shat on the things just washed. Their aim was too good. I flicked the dried pellet of faeces off with my nail and tried to ignore the stain of uric acid spreading outwards underneath. The interlacing of our world is getting stronger.

3

Wilding Clothes

Robert Bringhurst said "stories sprawl all over each other". So matted, so true. For five years I have been going in outdoor clothing shops and noodling on the back of an envelope the findings of a highly unscientific survey of how people dress when they go out 'in nature'. Around here at least and almost to a fault, people work footpath and bridleway, hill and dale dressed in polyester and nylon and lycra and goretex. The clothes of the outdoors are, it seems, oil-based. To wander the land, step one, don the by-products of petroleum. I laugh and then furrow my brow in turn at the confusion I feel. At how stories and products of synthetic chemistry sprawl all over lovers of the natural world.

Out in nature, it is good to be prepared. The message from the footpath travellers in the Peak District is that nothing says ready like a polyester fleece jacket and nylon-elastane blend trousers with zip-off legs. The question always hovering in my mind is: ready for what?

It seems to me that these outdoor wear garments have appeared in our wardrobes unconditionally, on their own initiative, as a given. That who knows when somewhere along the line a fleece was issued a free pass as regalia. And today it is *de rigueur*, beyond questioning, the dress entry requirement. These things are what you do when you do rambling. It is how you show that you're proficient. The pieces say I am able to stay out of trouble, I know about a compass, I have checked the weather forecast. They signal a knowledge of the hiking scene: how to fit in, how to put together a convincing ensemble, how to navigate a bog.

It's not the fact that there is an outdoor wear uniform that surprises me, but more that within it there's an obedient acceptance of certain fibres and articles of clothing as the items of preference. As garments go, there are few pieces less natural than a polyester fleece pullover. Nor are there many pieces that act to distance the world outside more than those made from filaments of hydrocarbon with their high resistance to micro-organisms, poor heat isolation and low water absorbency (hello polyester, hello nylon). A polyester base layer or a fleece jacket is drawn over the head consciously enough—of course it is, it is a strong, lightweight, durable garment—but the irony, does it register? Do we do it with a sardonic smile? The things we are wearing to arrive in nature do not, cannot, let nature in. We keep her at arm's length, or more literally sleeve's length, with hydrophobic fibres, an impervious fabric membrane and garments so durable they will outlive us all. Maybe this is the point of these pieces and I've just been slow to realise it. They're all about control and separation: when you seek out elemental nature, make sure to shield yourself from the elements; do some forest bathing, but only when the rain can't get in.

No one wants to be wet and cold while out and about or weighed down with heavy, sodden garments. No one wants to be saddled with endless laundry, trailing mud. Emphatically, lightweight clothes and waterproofs are a wonderful invention. Waterproofs with awareness of their effects, even better. It has always been the case that clothes, like many other things, mediate our experiences. That they strongly relate to the idea of being in nature and also to its opposite, human estrangement from nature and wilderness. For this reason alone it seems to me that it is important that we wear them with a fuller consciousness of how they influence our experiences. Maybe to question a given, especially such a common sensible one like to wear a fleece on a hike, we have to become insensible to common things. My friend Karen told me of two of her acquaintances who went on a skiing trip in a camper van. After a few days the smell in the van was revolting, gut churning, and they had to empty it, looking for the culprit. It turned out to be polyester base layers.

For the writer Barry Lopez, clothing is an equivalent of immersion in the natural world. He says, "Being out on the land is a state of mind. All of one's faculties are brought to bear in an effort to become fully incorporated into the land-scape. It is more than listening or watching, it is more than an analysis of what one senses. It is to have the land around you like clothing. To engage in a wordless dialogue with it."[2] I note that he says wordless, not mindless. Clothes as a way into the world. Clothes as an enveloping, an enabling, sensory voyage. From his work I like him so much. I wish he'd said which garments.

The confluence of social, cultural and technological forces that shapes how we live includes a drift away from the land to more of an indoor existence. It also includes an increasing specialisation of goods where every activity has its own suite of dedicated products set within an increasingly engorged consumer culture. Is this the root of the problem? With more indoor living comes more distance from nature and less familiarity and skill in the outdoors? With less knowledge of what to expect 'out there', we defer to professionals and their expert goods. And then we wander the hills; all the gear, no idea. This begs many questions, including: can you be prepared without the kit? Can you enter the wild with it? Yes and yes, I am sure that both and more are possible. It seems to me that to dwell better in the world, the first requirement is that we get outside, however we're dressed. Once we're there, we learn from the land and listen to the voices of the birds and the rain. We give attention to the untamed parts of our world, including that part in ourselves. We become more attuned. And this requires, at the least, that we make the layers that we build up around ourselves—some of which are fashioned in cloth—more permeable.

One of my pastimes is loitering on high streets looking at shops and people. Last year I stood for three half-hour periods at different times of the year outside a pair of shops in the market town of Hawes in North Yorkshire. Both stores are outdoor clothing retailers, but that's where the similarity ends. Cunningham's sells to tourists, to walkers; Walton's of Hawes, to the hunting and fishing set. In the windows of one are waterproofs, fleece jackets, map holders, Nordic walking poles and a dangling display of silver foil-insulated sitting mats. In the other, tweed plus fours, waxed jackets, a stuffed pheasant and neatly rolled cravats. Look one way and there is a colour palette of neon brights and black, saturated hues of pink, purple, cyan. Look the other, and it is muted green and brown, a little dusky orange. Outside, I wait to see if anyone goes into both stores. Barely a soul. A handful of crossovers only; visitors I think. They don't come out carrying a thing. Hunting-fishing-shooting gear versus walking gear: draw a Venn diagram of the offering of the two and there'd be nothing in the lozenge-shaped section in the middle save a rubber boot. To me this seems bizarre. Both shops sell kit for the same land, weather, purpose; but the logic is totally different. Store to store, the pieces have their own wildly different forms, like the beaks of Darwin's finches on neighbouring islands in the Galapagos. As I walk the ten paces between the two, the wet-weather offer shapeshifts between a triple layered nylon technical jacket and wax coatings, densely woven fabrics, hairy woollen cloth.

Class politics definitely draws the divide between the shops' stock and their audiences. On the right, the land owners; on the left, the landless. The gentry, with their country pursuits, versus the proletariat, with theirs. But the customer base is also segmented in other ways within these bald class groupings. They are also split along the lines of outdoor recreationist versus outdoor worker. No farm worker or builder I know would use an extendable walking ski pole or one of those fleece head bands that keeps ears warm. Nor would they wear a hiking cagoule. Too flimsy. Yet a rambler snaps them up. Confusingly, a farm worker also dresses like a country squire in a moleskin trouser and a tweed jacket for a trip to town, to be smart. But unlike the shooting party, he wears the tweed indoors, not out. Then there are others amongst us who casually wander up mountainsides in white trainers and tight jeans in the rain. Where do they fit in to all of this?

I am just happy that people are outside. But I'd also like it if things would cross-fertilise. I think we need some hybrid vigour. I remember the poet Gary Snyder, extending some thoughts of Thoreau's, once wrote about a crab apple, a tree that is part cultured, part wild. He said, "To go back to the wild is to become sour, astringent, crabbed. Unfertilized, unpruned, tough, resilient and every spring shockingly beautiful in bloom."[3] He was describing a culture-nature hybrid where the sharpness and shocking beauty of the world coalesce. A hybrid which bleeds through seams, races into a weave, labours into a garment's cut and into an integrated relationship with the natural world. This is how I want to dress. A wardrobe that welcomes wildness.

Walking in Skirts

I remember as a teenager that my paternal grandfather once said, "women with skirts up can run faster than men with trousers down" as a sexist joke. He often liked to rehearse his views that women and men were unequal. For instance, when I talked about following my older brother to university, he told me to know my place. Working the cash register in a shop, he said, was good work for girls, as he ordered me into the kitchen to wash the dishes. The "skirts up" one-liner was, I think, the only time, directly or indirectly, he ever alluded to sex in my earshot. Perhaps that is why it stayed with me. That and because aside from the chauvinism, the quip belies a literal truth: speedy, easy movement in skirts is real. Legs pivot at the hips and hinge at the knees and thus the speed of gait and fluidity of movement is massively eased by a wrap of fabric that skims the pelvis and falls loosely around the legs. That much I'll give him.

Walking, and sometimes running, in the hills in a skirt is a revelation. It is an exercise in rare freedom. I urge you to try it. Trousers can bunch and pull on the thighs, reining in the limbs and muscles; but a skirt is all space. A skirt is a modest, but as commodious, version of a birthday suit. It seems to me that a skirt also holds promise of a different sort of natural understanding: the same stretch of land seems altered when you navigate it in a skirt, you notice different things about it. A skirt is a kaleidoscope, it brings new things into view. Isn't that what we need? To see the world more fully?

It goes without saying that not all skirts enable unencumbered stepping. Scottish clans knew this and the pleated kilt is perhaps the obvious model of an outdoor working, walking, running skirt. I don't own a kilt. But I do have other skirts and dresses and they have granted me an education in both natural features and ergonomics.

The first thing I learned is linked to skirt length. For me, wearing a skirt in the hills that falls way below the knee is like wearing a blind fold: exciting but dangerous. I have fallen over and slipped and tripped many times because my boots blithely strike out over invisible ground, cloaked by the folds of my skirt. The cloaking effect happens especially when walking up hill or climbing over a wall when the distance from waist to ground shortens and the skirt's fabric pools forward; gravity acting to cascade it downwards and directly in the line of sight of the feet. To avoid this you need a spare hand to hoik the skirt up, or a fastening of some sort to gather up the fabric length on a climb. Or just a shorter skirt. So it is that topography draws skirt length. In flat lands, long skirts are A-OK. For hills, take out the scissors and hem your dress higher.

The second thing is related to a skirt's fullness. It is almost impossible to walk fast and loose if stride length is curtailed. A skirt with a small circumference, as measured at the hem, forces a tottering step. Sometimes this may be desired. But its disadvantages seem to be exaggerated outside a level, paved environment of a bar, a dancefloor, or a city. But if your preference is for all-terrain walking and running, this demands a skirt of a stride-length-and-a-bit as the bare minimum for fullness. Given that all legs are different lengths, this measurement varies. But the bit extra is essential for the moments where a bound, not just a step, is required. I once forded a shallow river in a skirt, leaping between stones. As I shaped to jump onto the far bank, the limits of the A-line skirt's cone shaped silhouette girdled my legs and I fell in. I needed more fabric in the flare. I probably needed pleats. That said, generous pleating is not the only precondition for easy walking. I have calculated that for me to avoid a hobbled stride, the minimum angle of flare necessary for a knee-length skirt made from a woven, non-stretch fabric is 58°. It's a reckoning contingent on many factors, not least whether a skirt has a split, and the likelihood of any route offering the opportunity for long, languid strides (my favourite type). In my experience long strides are inevitable when walking downhill. This makes the maxim: the tighter the contour lines, the looser the skirt. Or let the skirt decide. Tight skirt? Flat path.

An in-motion body is also influenced by a dress or skirt's cloth and garment construction. A knitted fabric, perhaps with added elastane, does away with much of the constricted movement of a tight skirt in a woven cloth. This opens the door to a figure-hugging but limber walking silhouette. For fabric with little give, good pattern cutting, including well-placed darts and pleats, is an ally of ready movement. My interest is in the clothes I already have, and most of mine fall into this latter category. I look at the skirts and dresses on my hanging rail in terms of capabilities, of what they will allow me to do, of how they might expand real freedoms. I also consider them in light of the weather. Will they keep me warm enough or too hot? How will they cope in a breeze? A strong wind plays havoc with a full skirt.

At midsummer a few years ago I walked for a week in the northernmost part of Sweden, on a route across an exquisite area of tundra inside the arctic circle. Before I left I asked Ingun, a Norwegian friend of mine, well used to the far north, what she would recommend I wear. Smart as a whip she replied a skirt, a silk skirt. I wasted no time and rifled through my chest of drawers for something suitable. Her thinking was that such an item was light in a rucksack, it packed down small, and silk dries fast. Besides it meant that layers could be added or removed as the temperature dictated without fully stripping off and waterproof trousers could be pulled on quickly in a sharp shower yet still the outfit would not get too bulky or hot. In my wardrobe I found a bias cut silk dress from the 1950s that had been my grandma's. It was a delicate beige with an orange and mid brown irregular stripe. The fabric was thin and torn in places and I decided to cut across the bodice to make a skirt, adding a wide elasticated waistband and darts, and to shorten it a little, to sit just below the knee. On the first day of the trip I put the skirt on over thick woollen leggings. It was an unusual get up, like a babushka or an onion. Layers of hand-me-down woollen jumpers, a scarf, leggings and old silk. When she saw me, Karen, the friend who I was walking with, was laughing and disbelieving. What was my motivation she wanted to know? Was I trying to get attention, to flirt, to pull? I insisted that the skirt was practical; practical not sexual. She raised an eyebrow. She did not know about walking in skirts. I think she took the skirt as a sign that I wasn't serious about the trip. That my mind was elsewhere. And in some ways she was right. I was the opposite of serious. I was easy and spacious and free. I was walking in a skirt.

5

Birds

I was sitting on a low rock beneath a young pine. At the top of the tree, on a dead silvered branch, was a bald eagle. To my back, the Pacific Ocean broke onto a low cliff; its lapping, stroking sound was everywhere. After a while, the eagle, all strong bands of colour, rose up and heavily flew away. Where she soared, my eyes followed hypnotically. Fully stretched, the wings of a bald eagle arc slightly forward, their leading edge forging a gentle curve, her head the only thing to interrupt the sweep. You'd imagine that wings in a forward arc would cup the air, add drag and hold the bird back. It shows how little I know.

In this same part of Vancouver Island on Canada's westernmost fringe, a bald eagle has been spotted repairing to its nest with a t-shirt. Was it (I fill in the gaps for no one knows) a band t-shirt? Did she get it at a gig? Nick it from a washing line? Or perhaps she rifled through a pile of surfer's clothes on a beach to find something she liked? Somewhere here or hereabouts, two hundred grams of an eerie is cotton single jersey. I love this story. It assigns us as part of the same ecosystem. Eagles in t-shirts: we are all in this together.

Several years ago I read J. A. Baker's sublime 1967 account of a winter spent watching and following peregrine falcons around the coast of Kent in southeast England. The opening pages offer up a description of contrasts between a picture of the peregrine, like you'd find in a spotters guide, and actual experience of the living bird:

> *"Books about birds show pictures of the peregrine...*
> *Large and isolated in the gleaming whiteness of the*

page, the hawk stares back at you, bold, statuesque,
brightly coloured. But when you have shut the book,
you will never see that bird again... The living bird
will never be so large, so shiny-bright. It will be deep
in landscape, and always sinking further back...
Pictures are waxworks beside the passionate mobility
of the living bird." [4]

Baker, I think, was preparing his readers for the t-shirt-eagle whole. He was saying that rich, bountiful understanding comes from knowing things against a backdrop of other things as they happen in the real world. He was saying that a thing is known better when known within its context; that we must guard against a tendency to make things simpler by separating them out, because separation lessens them. Things are greater when they're understood in relationship: bird to place, person to land, garment to the real world.

I read Baker's book during a spring while my family and I were living in a converted farm outbuilding called Woodcutter's Cottage. Swallows started arriving in late April and built nests in the barn beneath the room where we slept. Their chatter—like the radio tuning dial turning through static—was in every moment, was part of my days and nights. They hardly rested. I have no idea how they coped. The surprising news from the farm, given that swallows are birds of such wingsmanship, of great migration, was that they also sit down. Granted they perch most often in nests and on phone lines, but one evening when the cloud rolled back and the sky cleared, out of the cottage window my youngest son saw a swallow sitting on the ground. Alert but entirely motionless on one of yard's stone flags, facing into a shaft of low light from the setting sun. Then we saw another, a couple of paces away from the first, settled, still, perfectly parallel to the first, facing west. I'd never seen a swallow on the ground before, let alone there and stationary. They were warming their brick-coloured throats in the rays of evening light.

In our summer together, the swallows found a use for me. I became part of their ecosystem. News of my status as a magnet for biting insects had got out. At the edge of Macclesfield forest, I would be followed around by a massive vertical bloom of midges which would first gather and then descend. I tried a couple of times to relax, to let them bite. It was excruciating. The bite of single midge is almost imperceptible, the prick of a tiny pin. But their numbers and insatiability would drive me crazy. They were in my ears, eyes, nose, my skin and scalp, crawling, I pressed my lips together tight. Then, a rush of air against my cheek. The swallows arrived, scything, ravaging the midge bloom.

At Woodcutter's Cottage there were birds everywhere. The sky was continuously moving, flecked with darting flurries of feather and beak. When we first moved to the cottage, I studied books to help me identify the birds, but these quickly fell out of use. They didn't help much. They rarely showed birds in flight or in mixed groups, or in habitats or from the angles I saw. The books just didn't capture my experience of the birds around me. There was nothing in those pages about how flocks of goldcrest move like loose schools of butterflies high in the forest canopy, or about the likeness of the tails and flight of skylarks and chaffinches twirling around as the car flushes them out of the verge. Nor do they say that the greater spotted woodpecker strikes the bird feeder like keys on a typewriter, hammers a headline and punctuates it with a warning peep. She is a very correct creature, deportment excellent, navigating the bird table leg at right angles. All the while her two young roll around on the grass, squabbling and play fighting like lion cubs. When does one become the other? The juvenile become the adult, and trade rolling around for standing up straight? The pages don't say. They don't tell me why a single snow bunting is living on the lane, way off course, and whether it is lonely. Nor do they prepare me for the feeling of living close to nesting kestrels. The kestrels are at the gable end of one of the barns, with four huge grey chicks. Any human presence in the farmyard flushes the parents out. Their route from the nest is always the same. They head west, skirting the copse, below the height of the tree canopy. Then they bank sharply right, where the wind tips the birds high, fast, out of view.

With time I learnt the birds' names but only after I learnt their haunts and ways of moving, their calls, their markings, their peculiar habits and how they made me feel. Like Nan Shepherd says, "[wo]man's experience of them enlarges rock, flower and bird. The thing to be known grows with the knowing".[5] It is the same for clothes: fashion, like ornithology, is enriched by direct experience. We know them both better because they are alive in the endless variation of the contexts in which we experience them. We know them better when we replace the abstract idea we have about a garment, a bird, with its actual worldly reality. When we trade the magazines and the celebrity outfits for lived experience.

What the birds taught me was that better understanding requires a commitment of alertness. It was almost that straightforward. In order to grow an understanding of the world, I had to notice more, to be drawn in, sucked in, in order to be opened out, to be able to see. The life of our clothes is a story of integrated relationships. To try to understand a garment apart from its background is to risk the collapse of both. To be what they are, they require each other.

In the north of Norway I heard about wild eiders. In spring some of these shy ducks build a nest in small 'houses' next to human ones. A few of these duck houses are purpose built (I saw one on Google that looked like a fancy dog kennel), others are more ad hoc—a bucket on its side. When in situ, the eiders preen and tease the softest down from their breasts and work them into a crown-shaped nest the size of a dinner plate. While the eggs are being incubated, the local people have to move about quietly and put off any noisy tasks, as the birds are easily disturbed. But move about they must, for human presence is what the birds are seeking to keep predators away.

When the young fledge, the house is abandoned. The down nest, the highly prized filling of clothes and bedding, is gathered up and normal human life resumes. Chainsaws, drum practice, start up again. The down is traditionally cleaned with the aid of a special frame which looks a bit like a harp. The frame is balanced horizontally on a lap between the knees and the nest is placed on top. It is then plucked, strummed, the vibrations shaking out the dirt, separating leaf, dust and the feather light down. I can't help but think that this should be how all materials are made; out of a harp-frame song of partnership.

When I was working on projects in Finland in the hot 'climate summer' of 2018, I stayed in a cabin next to a lake. The water was warm, rippling, fringed with trees. Once when I was swimming, an arctic tern plucked a fish from the lake in front of me. For a moment, an instant, the water acting as a conductor, I imagined we touched. This made me ridiculously happy. And for the rest of my stay my swimming schedule was set by passing birds. I was born and raised in Liverpool (the city's emblem, lest we forget, is a bird), but my blood, like yours, is feathers. And my name, a reminder that birds are our heritage. A fletcher is a flight maker, working the arrow to fly straight and true.

6

Place of Origin

There was death this spring as well as life. Lambs were born and some died. Some ewes were still in shock days after lambing, dazed by birth. One of the lambs on the smallholding where we were living, a twin, was not getting enough milk—his mother had only one teat working after mastitis —and he was weak, cold. One evening, a crow, sensing the lamb's vulnerability, pecked out his eye, attacked his tongue, tore a gash by his tail and opened up his side. He was as good as dead when the farmer, Paddy, found him: limp, chilled, emaciated. My husband, still a vet but now working with computers, stitched his wounds with fishing line and cut up drinking straws to fashion an eye closure. We warmed him with hot water bottles. Paddy fed him through a tube. Somehow he survived. The kids named the one-eyed lamb Lucky the Pirate and he would charge the full length of the field to butt our legs and the bottle we fed him with.

In the days following Lucky's escape I noticed a crow patrolling the farmyard. He was statuesque and perfectly black except for a white patch of feathers just to the right of centre on his breast. I couldn't help myself: I imagined this is the one that went for Lucky and the patch of white was a little of Lucky made manifest in him. Aren't each of us, after all, a product of our experiences? The crow had a medal the colour of lamb-white on his chest: the scavenger general, splendid in his survival. As I watched him strut about I thought that this could be one of those moments that makes visible the web of relationships that we so rarely see. And then, as if to guard against any sentimentality that would rise within me as I warmed my fingers in Lucky's front legpit crease, in the tiny curls of fleece, I saw the local stoat criss-crossing the yard, this time with a mouse in his mouth. Another death, another meal, another loss-and-gain. And then Crow swooped on the stoat. He was almost mythical now this crow. Hungry, chancing his luck, instinctive.

The invisible web of relations span in my head. Perhaps it was because I was surrounded by sheep, by all that wool, but it seemed to me that there was something in the associations between the land and what goes on there that adjusts the experience of wearing clothes. Just as certain landscapes hold certain thoughts about the world, like they hold certain stones or plants, so they hold certain ideas about clothing. On the rough ground of the north of England the thoughts I have are of large pockets to carry tissues—my nose is always running; of clothes cut for the easy, swinging movement of legs and arms; of a generous hood to pull up against the wind; of layers, about three; and of an outfit with flashes of colour to signal to the birds that I see them and like how they dress.

Granted I know little about agriculture, but the land and sky around the farm where we were living—the soil, altitude, the levels of light, rainfall and temperature—govern what grows easily there. And that which does grow tells us about the particulars of shielding and protection, of adornment and fittingness of things—of us—to our surroundings. Hillsides, where the hardiest breeds of sheep graze year-round, say that wool wears well on this land. Likewise, the absence of a crop like cotton, surely tells us to forgo it as a wardrobe mainstay in a cool, damp clime. I think so. But perhaps I would say that. I am, how to say this, *preoccupied* by wool, by its complex, scaly fibre structure, by its durability, bulk, elasticity, moisture absorption and release, by its degree of natural stain resistance, and its ability to shrink if agitated when wet. Wool as a fibre calls into being particular ideas and behaviour with clothes. I like all this suggests: low maintenance, highly appreciated, strong, warm. Like a good man. Consider a woollen suit or cardigan, versus a formal cotton shirt, a pair of tracky bottoms. Do you feel different in them, act different? What's good for me is that this augury—the sheep and its fleece—is everywhere here. Wool is the Peak District's fibre crop. It is this landscape's fashion direction. It is also the only fibre that we can still process entirely within the shores of the UK. I am following its lead because it is suited here. I also like it, it becomes me. I want to be alert, adapted, as fleet of foot as a sheep on a fell. Read the landscape, tap into a place, know about it, how to move through it, how to navigate its social, cultural and natural flows and what it requires of us; and then we will thrive. It is what to wear in the midst of it all.

Yet after whiling away hours with the people who live in the closest town to the farm, Macclesfield, I see that wool isn't worn dependably here. In the Domesday Book (1086) the town is entered as "Macclesfeld", where 'feld' meant open country. In the thirteenth century much of Macclesfield's wealth was dependent on agriculture. Each 'burgess', an inhabitant with full rights of citizenship, was allotted an acre of land within town fields, the right to dig peat, and to pasture sheep, horses and cattle on the common land. Today however, such a history of wool manifests itself barely at all in the local collective wardrobe. I know there are many reasons for this, which include among other things: washing machines, cheapness of synthetic fibres, centrally heated homes, fashion culture; but it bothers me still. I thought perhaps it had something to do with novelty seeking, with fashion's obsession with the new, with 'originality', where wool is seen as 'old'. This reminded me of a lovely piece I once read which said that in the West, originality is considered to be something that has never been said or done before; whereas in indigenous cultures, it is understood differently, as an invitation to reconnect with the source of things, a deep place of origin. This makes originality something that takes place in accordance with 'original instructions'; an act or idea that starts with the land.[6]

In the summer after Lucky's close call, a local sheep farmer who doubles as a shearer came to the farm to clip the small flock of ewes and the two rams. The shears he brought to do the job were a crazily horned, oversized version of the clippers you find in a high street barbershop. He oiled them generously, hung them on a pole, they looked like a weapon of torture. He was a giant of a man and worked deftly and with tenderness towards the animals, his spine curving into a dome to accommodate the difference in size between him and the beasts. I asked him, a man literally knee-deep in wool, and dependent on it for his living, whether he ever wore it. "No". Do you ever eat lamb? I asked. "Don't like it much".

It is as the news reports say. It costs more to pay the shearer than you can earn from selling the clipped fleece of upland cross-bred sheep. There is no market for it; mixed grade raw wool is almost without value. Shearing has become a farm husbandry issue whereas it used to be a route to a valuable asset. Paddy stuffs the clipped fleece in a couple of huge sacks and they sit in the yard, weighed down by stones. This is where we are.

Yet it's not like this in pockets of Shetland. I visited in the autumn after Lucky's birth. In Shetland, wool is worn, talked about and seen as alive. I saw a car mechanic lively in it underneath his overalls; young men in the pub, the teller in the post office, vibrant. I met the bear-like foreman of a wool sorting shed with lanolin soft hands who talked about wool in active voice. Wool, alive, because sheep graze and grow on pasture in the sun and rain confers it with the active principles of life. In Shetland, children practice knitting in school. The motifs they learn are handed down through families like a photo album. The patterns are named after the print a wave makes on a sandy shore; after a ram's horn. It is vital matter, in all senses of the word. The fibres are livelihood for many on the island. They keep the body temperature of people who live there a little higher. They signal belonging. They look grand in the island's clear light, when leading towards the origins.

7

Change and Permanence

It was the 8th of May, and it was the day that the forest floor and canopy, sliding their own colour gradients, merged. This was the day they became the exact same shade of green. I'd been holding out for weeks, watching the colours of Macclesfield Forest ripen and alter, rationalising, diversifying, rising taller. When it came, the total effect was like immersion into a dreamscape of haze and indistinct edges. The windless-ness helped, low down on the slope off a main track: the air was still, hovering, vibrating at the frequency of green.

My overwhelming sense of the forest's top-to-bottom green was that it was deeply relaxing. Part of me marvelled at the exact synchronicity of hue, while another part looked around for where I might sleep. In the days following the 8th, the effect dissipated, less potent than before. The collective floor-bound plants, a tangle of bramble, grass, moss, leaves of wild flowers, travelled from fervent green towards a less energetic green-grey; while in the tree canopy high above, the needles of the predominant species—larch—toughened, darkened, became harder, more mahogany. Never before had I seen so clearly how each element of the forest runs its own course. Nor how sometimes the elements intersect, momen-tarily, blissfully crossing. As they did, the forest seemed to rouse itself, flexing, moving, at a wavelength of around 550 nanometres in the spectrum of visible light. The American writer Barry Lopez puts it this way: "The land becomes large, alive like an animal. It is not that the land is simply beautiful, but that it is powerful."[7]

There are so many unfolding courses, paths and routes in the forest, of creatures, of colour, of plants, going off in different directions, that it is always surprising to me that I witness any of their comings together at all. They remind me of a map in Denis Woods's book *Everything Sings* that shows the delivery route that a paperboy takes in town. His route is drawn as a ribbon that zig zags left-right around a neighbourhood, plotting his path in space. Yet the ribbon is also stretched out, vertically elongated, as it charts the paperboy's route over time. The result is a map that looks like a party streamer, bouncy and spiralling, running above the streets, up the page. My sense when I look at it is of how open-ended places become when time is factored in, of how much roomier they turn out to be; of how time spreads space with possibilities. It makes a fleeting beautiful moment, like total forest green, feel more special, like fortune. Yet it also makes it one moment among many. The endless recombination of elements over time in which all manner of novelties are being continuously launched into the world.

The moment where time and space converge is also something I have witnessed in an outfit: the point when person, place and dress come together and speak the language of now. A fashion moment, like a forest moment, is an electric experience, unpredictable, unschooled, emergent. A navy sleeveless crossover blouse, loose fitting; high waisted trousers, also deep blue with square cut pocket openings; old trainers; a day and a night where life sings. I see from Denis Woods's space-time ribbon map something I'd not seen so clearly before. Time also expands garments' possibilities; it spreads them like water. It peels the three spatial dimensions of a garment off the peg, and drapes it around an ever-changing, unfolding, animate life. Woods's map, if it were about clothes, would say that garments are lived as a process. That lives happen within them; that clothes unfold along the dimension of time. The time-space ribbon would also say that garments are crucibles of action, time designating them wide open to all manner of intersecting forces. Just like in the forest. To witness both a forest and a fashion moment demands our time and attention, a showing up on our part. It also implies return; that we turn up, dress up, over and again.

The edge of the forest was visible from upstairs in Woodcutter's Cottage where we'd been living in between other homes. My things and a desk were set up next to a window. Outside the window, pheasants barked, light gathered in pools, and the wide and deep landscape revealed it all: change and permanence, the objective reality of our planet.

The cottage was about a mile from the nearest road and the lane that linked us was steep and full of bends, like a fairground ride. At the lane's edge was coarse grass and broken drystone walls. Brown hares lived here. They ran along the lane. They legged it in the late afternoon, at dusk and at night in the tunnel of light thrown out by our car's main beam. Their movement was pleasure and ease, the hinging and folding of limbs, feet, independent ears swivelling, listening. One evening as I drove home, I watched one streak ahead of our car and then without warning, she leaped into the verge and stopped instantly. She sniffed the air and turned. We looked at each other, I did not blink, held in the strange bondage of the eyes. Gaze still locked together, slowly I eased the car past. In my rear view mirror I watched her saunter back the way she had come. She lived as she should, as I should, true to her experience; choosing her route with a keen and fierce will.

After a morning of rain I went into the forest and as I crossed into a dense stand of conifers, I was embraced by dark air and heavy drizzle. To the sides and before the copse it was bright, lovely, humid. But inside it was raining. The trees dropped hours' old water on me from above: large, fat, slow blobs, falling in a dense screen. All around the conditions had changed, yet what had gone before still lingered. The lag in the system slows our experience of things shifting. But it is coming.

8

The Wind

Today I wanted to go to the Goyt Valley. I was late leaving and missed the best of the bright skies. I was irritated by the turn in the weather, by the fact that I hadn't come sooner. But I was already bent out of shape, frustrated. I knew in part what it was: my youngest son was nine today and for me a set of deep, primal emotions are stirred on the birthday of one of my children. I was batey because the intensity of such feelings is private, they are experienced alone, no one else holds them or advocates for them, just their owner; and I had only left myself the scrag-end of the day.

In the Goyt Valley, the day's scrag-end was cool and wind screamed from the west. The cloud base, total grey, flattened the landscape. As I walked, the clouds lowered still more and it began to rain, the unceasing fine rain of an autumn low-pressure system. I climbed through the trees to the high ridge, edging a wall and on to the open moorland. The wind, howling across the Dark Peak was now at my back. I scuttled along in the cloud mist, my feet doing tiny racing steps, tottering, jerky, not my own.

It was then that I felt it. The wind, holding me. There is no better way to describe it. It came careening up and over the moor, leaning into me, pressing into me and it lodged itself there. The touch of the wind that day is best explained not by measures of force or speed, but by its quality: steady, a constant pressure, like a solid, a person touching you. No raggedy unevenness of blustery gusts, the air was dependable under my limbs. It had an edge—a form—I could feel it, like the urge of an arm, a body, close at my back. The wind filled the underside of my mittens, pooled at the back of my coat, under my hood, the legs of my trousers ballooning forward like sails. Together we stumbled the ridge. Each step I took the holding reorganised itself around my body, spooning me. It knew who I was. For how else to explain that as I moved, it was already there, filling in the space where I was not: a remarkable, anticipatory, physical presence. It was, I think, the feeling of being held by so perceptive a force, by something so participatory, that made me cry. A bend of air found me strewn on a hillside and attended to me. Nothing was asked for in return.

Still entangled, the wind and I blew into a hollow just off the path and as I scrambled out and onto higher ground, I disturbed red grouse, seven of them. They took flight and split up, cackling under the exertion of their panicked wingbeats. I turned my face into the gale to watch them go. Not only had the wind said lean on me, it had also divulged one of the best tricks of stalking.

Three weeks later I go back to the same area with my oldest boy. We walk together, sometimes side-by-side, but mostly I am behind, he being at the age where he runs everywhere. On the far hills, the rough land of the moor is purple, the bare stems of heather in winter, and blue, the underside of pine needles. The cloud is still low—it hasn't lifted for weeks—but in the wind everything pulses.

As we skirt another high ridge, the wind blows across and through us, piling in just behind the left shoulder seam and forcing its way out at the collarbone, centre right. As we reach the highest part of the ridge, exposed fully, we skitter, scudder along, our bodies moving compulsorily in the charge of air. Out of control legs, we laugh and stumble, my coat's sleeves bow in the gusts, making the bones in my arms into shapes never before seen in a limb. I look at them, these crazy, soft, alien distortions. I like the new me. We throw ourselves down on the bilberry shrub floor, flattening ourselves into the ground, raucous, giddy. We lift our heads, our arms, again my mittens fill with air; the wind is holding my hand. My coat's wide sleeves grip onto the lip of a gust, my trousers, wide-legged act as a kite. These are the key pieces of the season. And if you have a top layer that opens up the front, so much the better. To hold and be held, undo the fastening, grasp the bottom corners, one in each hand, and then gripping your coat tight, raise your arms high above your head.

Jumper

I sat swaddled in the jumper my dad has worn continuously for more than fifty years and lifted a pen. I daubed my lips with a smudge of red lipstick and then self-consciously blotted it away. What was I doing? I had no idea if was even possible to write about kinship between clothing, people and the natural world; to tell stories of garments made whole by their surroundings. As I sat, warm, in a sweater distorted by my father's body and by sawdust and toil, I looked down. The jumper, knitted in three shades of undyed brown wool, were the same colours as in my hair.

I felt my cheeks flush, an adrenalin spike of surprise.

> "This quiet ritual took place on the very edge of the world I see, very near to the world beyond the looking glass, the lost place, the beginning of things." [8]

I fidgeted uncomfortably, I was skittish. I really had never noticed before. I was undone by a sensation of fleeting, rushing recognition; by a feeling of almost understanding, by a connection with a jumper. And then it was gone, as quickly as it had come, out of my grasp. I was left stranded, with little idea about what it meant. My eyes darted to the window, looking for escape. I forced myself to look again at my hair splayed over the jumper's shoulders, but my brain, raking over things, was looking at itself thinking, trying too hard. The plug had already been pulled. I had no idea how to proceed and so I gave up with the pen and sloped off.

I can't remember a time when this jumper was anything other than my favourite of dad's knitwear. My grandma bought it for him before he went to sea as a ship's second engineer in 1963. He sailed back and forth between the UK and the Pacific coast of South America on a merchant ship. It transported engineering supplies on the outward leg and a hold full of guano on the return. I always liked that last part, it seemed a ridiculous cargo, it must have stunk, much like the madness of industrial agriculture. That was in a distant age before he grew a beard. We have never known him without it or the jumper.

I also coveted a v-neck cardigan of his which was cut like a jacket. It was from the same period of the sixties as the jumper. It was made from fine gauge knitted panels with contrast piping, two shallow pockets at waist level and faux leather buttons. It hung for a long time on a peg in his workshop. But the jumper is different. I have a photo of him from 1965 wearing it when on holiday with his mates on the Isle of Skye in Scotland. Then through the nineteen seventies, eighties, nineties, noughties it crops up over and again in the family album. My dad, my siblings and I—mere mortals—age, allowing me to date each shot, but the jumper itself seems above all that.

The background in these photos is almost always the landscape of northern English fells: hill country, rough, hard, bleak. My family has been visiting the western side of the Yorkshire Dales for decades to stay in a battered stone house on the side of a fell. The house, Thrushgill, named after a stream, is often in shot. That my dad wore the jumper there is testament to its qualities: high crimp, long, coarse fibres, an insulating barrier against wind and cold. It wore him too. In the years of my life I have watched it wear him old and mellow. He's always been kind. It wore him softer and wiser, practically skilful and strong through his work in timber, plumbing pipes and stone. And then later, some of his strength transferred into his easy chuckle after his left shoulder's tendons snapped when he lifted a huge boulder into a wall.

The jumper is these places: limestone, larch trees, crimson-berried hawthorn, rushes, streams, flocks of thrush. And who he is there: practical, pared back, happy. It has become an agent for the collective place, its weather, the surfaces around, the people who live alongside. Though that is not where my dad or I grew up. We were born and raised in the middle of Liverpool, in terraced houses with small concrete 'yards' at the back, boxed in by high brick walls. No birds, no greenery, no long view. And yet by some feat, the jumper acts as a portal and propels him and me both into a parallel reality. He asked me recently if I'd brought the jumper with me when we went to Thrushgill together. "To fit in" he said, and I realised that he saw it this way too.

Dad's jumper is patched at the elbows, splashed with paint, repaired. Earlier today I spent another hour darning more holes in it. I borrowed it from him under the guise of mending it, though really my motive was more complicated. It's always been a charm for me. I needed it close. I wanted to wear it, to write in it. I needed the help.

The new holes only became noticeable after I washed it. Life and grime must have held it together; it was at least a decade since it had last seen a sink. I wasn't bothered about the dirt. Or the smell, in fact, I liked it. But the ribbed waist-band was massively distorted, kicking out like a skirt. It needed warmth and water to help it relax. The hand washing was momentous. Two sink-fulls of soapy water followed by four clean baths to rinse. It was caked—festooned—with everything. I wondered if I should try to capture the waste-water's colour somehow but it was a momentary thought and it came to me only when I was elbow-deep in the sink. Though I regret it now. It was a shade of warm, liquid brown, like fine cocoa with a glassy sheen.

The mending repair took many different approaches, some from the underside, others from the face. I darned to close large holes, working in a spiral from outside in. I hand felted two sections of the left sleeve using hedgerow wool that I picked from barbed wire fences and rough tree trunks that sheep use as scratching posts. I worked the mended sections with additional weaving stitches in the three-colour vertical dogtooth pattern, chocolate, bronze-brown, cream-grey. The flecked dark brown Shetland wool in my needle followed the grid lines. As I worked my lap felt warm. Doing this felt like a way to live not just through the rules of modern society.

I wore dad's jumper in the high Atacama desert in northern Chile. I was at a gathering of indigenous Aymara weavers, woman mainly, who work on backstrap looms, interlacing the fibre that they first collect and then spin from their own herds of llama and alpaca on the high plateau. The gathering started with a ceremony of blessing and gratitude, with music, dancing and eating and then a weaving competition. We made flags. Later we told stories of clothes, and dad's jumper and its five decades of continuous use was unremarkable there. It was a place of innate natural understanding. Every potato the Aymara plant, every animal they care for, every length of fabric they weave is seen as part of the basic cell of life. There were no divisions between things. Nothing was dealt with singly. Everything understood in relation to something else. While there, I was interviewed by a journalist from a local newspaper who photographed me smiling-grimacing through altitude sickness at 4500m. In the snap, I am wearing the jumper. The mountains are all around.

NOTES

1. Erika Hasebe-Ludt, Cynthia M. Chambers, and Carl Leggo, *Life Writing and Literary Métissage as an Ethos for Our Times* (New York: Peter Lang Publishing, 2009) p.129.
2. Barry Lopez, *Arctic Dreams* (London: The Harvill Press, 1986) p.199.
3. Gary Snyder, *The Practice of the Wild* (Berkeley: Counterpoint, 1990) p.190.
4. J. A. Baker, *The Peregrine* (New York: New York Review Books, 1967) p.19.
5. Nan Shepherd, *The Living Mountain* (Edinburgh: Canongate Books, 2011) p.108.
6. Glenn Aparicio Parry, 'Think of Time as Nature Thinks' (*Resurgence*, 294, 2016) pp.21–24.
7. Barry Lopez, ibid. p.392.
8. J. A. Baker, ibid.

ACKNOWLEDGEMENTS

To Louise St Pierre, Katelyn Toth-Fejel, Anna Fitzpatrick
and Katherine Pogson, I live in gratitude for your reading,
your caring and for making me bolder. My thanks to Charlie
Meecham for the photographs and for walking with me in
the winter. To the *Lady of Avenel* and sailors on the voyage
What Has To Be Done?: this began aboard, thank you all. To
Hardingland Paradise where it continued and my friends
there, and you, Lime Tree, I am forever grateful. They were
ten months that changed things. Then to Lohja and Elisa,
where it restarted, *kiitos*. And to my folks and my boys:
these are our real lives. For them I am always grateful.

Afterword

Photographs of Macclesfield Forest and the Goyt Valley in the Peak District and Garsdale in the Yorkshire Dales by Charlie Meecham.